STOP RENTING
and be a homeowner NOW!!

Jay CREATES homeowners!!

Table of Contents

WHY Are You STILL Renting?

You can become a homeowner, by the end of this month, with one phone call!

This one action can make you a homeowner, if you just follow the simple steps detailed in this amazing book. These steps have helped countless others become happy, excited, homeowners - in some cases with just one phone call!!! The information included here will show you with crystal clear directions how to have what the world calls "The American Dream," owning your own home. You know you have worked hard all of your life and sometimes you say to yourself, "What do I have to show for it all?" Well, you no longer have to worry about that after reading this Book because the American Dream is at your fingertips. Believe me, you deserve to finally stop renting and enjoy the benefits of owning your own home.

There is nothing more intimidating than being in a crowd of all your homeowner friends who can't stop talking about the house they just bought and all the lovely perks that went with it. Like your buddy with the great yard by the brook, or your brother with the massive maple trees that surround his green manicured lawn. These guys don't know how lucky they have it when every morning they get up and enjoy a piping cup of hot coffee on their own back deck. All the while you're thinking, "Gosh, I have rented houses all my life; I sure wish I could own my OWN home." Now you can!!! Now, you can be that person who proudly talks about your new accomplishment of being a homeowner.

For all the hard work you have done in your life, you deserve to get to this point. You have accomplished something awesome!!! Your parents will be proud of you!! Your friends will be excited for you. You can share the feelings, the process, and the fulfillment with everyone you know and love. This is a big deal for you and you have earned this!

Look, the economy is tanked right now and renting is pretty common in most areas. Heck, think about who is in your circle of friends and family now. Just casually count how many are renters and how many are home owners. I bet a lot of them rent and may never have the opportunity you are getting right now to change that. They just don't know what they don't know.

Holy cow! I just thought of something. Maybe, just maybe, with the knowledge you have in your hands right now, you could not only become a homeowner, but you could share this secret with those you love and make a difference in their lives. I know that sharing and giving to others has brought a multitude of great fortunes to me. I also know if you are reading this, you are a person of action. I have no doubt that you are also a giver and care about other people, just like I do!

What I am about to share with you is not just a chance to have something to call your own, but an opportunity to become more confident and self-assured. This secret will provide you a reason to get up in the morning, look around and know you can get anything you want, just by following this simple plan. Information is everywhere and you are in the right place, at the right time, to finally stop renting and learn how to become a homeowner!!!! Congratulations.

Why Can't You Become a Homeowner?

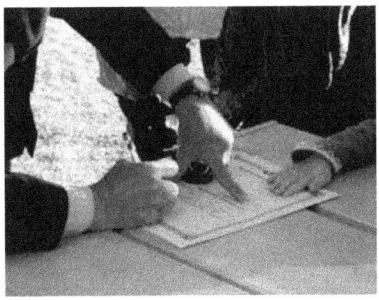

I can remember the first time one couple signed the paper work for their first home. They were ecstatic!! I could see the pride and sheer joy on their faces as they took turns signing the paperwork. For me, helping them achieve their goal was like watching my own child graduate, or accomplish something huge!

One client, who had rented apartments and houses all his life, told me how much respect he received from family members after he became the owner of his new home. He explained to me the feeling of accomplishment, the daily excitement that came from reaching his goal and from the knowledge that he did it for himself. For him, having that boost of respect and admiration must have made his victory all the sweeter.

Many customers of mine have gone on to share this technique of how to become a homeowner with others. They have been through the process with me and had such success for themselves, they could not wait to share it with their friends and family. This alone has value. Now, they pass on this knowledge to help others fulfill their, American Dream.

One customer from Moira, NY used this proven method to purchase his family's dream home, a four bedroom farmhouse with a beautiful front porch. The property included a gigantic barn that had a massive storage space above the garage, all this in a quiet country setting and on a great street. Their kids now play in a spacious back yard they can call their own. The

new owners are now free to improve it the just the way they want, and you know what? They did! They added on a room, just the way they wanted it! No landlord to tell *them* what to do.

There are countless stories I can tell you about the confidence homeowners have gained by becoming just that - a *home owner* the way I will show you in this Book.

The transformation that I witnessed in one Massena, NY homeowner was astounding! He told me how owning his own house made him more responsible in other areas of his life as well. He now took more action on following through with things such as bill paying, upkeep and making sure things get done around the house. I know what you're thinking - *"bill paying and cleaning the house is not what I want to think of"*!!! Well, let me ask you these questions. How do you <u>feel</u> when all your bills are paid? Come on, really <u>feel</u> it. How do you <u>feel</u> when your house is organized, neat and clean? I bet if you really visualize this happening, and I promise you it will, you will feel *fantastic*! You will feel *accomplishment*. I have faith in you. You can do this.

I have acquired many, many homes and properties with the strategy I am about to explain. You can become an American Dream Home owner with this advice. Already own your own home? Then you can become a Real Estate investor with this information. This step by step path is a way to overcome the obstacles of 20% down payments the bank requires of you. Heck, we go to the bank to borrow money and they are asking us to have money first? You don't need 20% down! Ask any of my countless customers if what you are about to learn has helped them, and you will get an astounding, "Absolutely

YES!! I recommend buying a house from Jay with this strategy."

This Book will help thousands of people, just like you, learn how to finally make a house, your home. All you have to do is follow my plan and, once and for all, you can grab hold of the "American Dream". Take action now on what I tell you here and I promise you will not regret it!! Now go get it!!! I am excited for you.

I DON'T WANT TO RENT ANYMORE!

Have you ever been a renter? Well, I have and I know how you feel. By not owning my own property or having the "American Dream" I had this feeling that dug at every part of my being. When I was young and just starting out, just like some of you, I was a renter. Perhaps there is a time in life when renting is a great idea, maybe when you are "up in age" and maintaining a property is a burden, but I'm talking about first time ownership here. Renting an apartment as a full-fledged adult, moving out of your parents' house is an awesome feeling. You have freedom. Fast forward a couple of years and think of how you have said to yourself, *"Boy, I wish I could own my own house."* You have thoughts of a big house with all kinds of rooms and a kitchen where the whole family can sit and just be happy. For me, I imagined a family Thanksgiving Day with all of my loved ones enjoying a great home cooked meal.

I don't have to tell you the downsides of renting. Perhaps, you have had an experience or two that sticks in your mind, like when the septic system was not adequate and the toilets overflowed, or the landlord would not schedule routine maintenance on the plumbing and your whole kitchen flooded due to a sink trap that malfunctioned. All these scenarios are just some of the headaches and frustrations of renting. Well, you might say, if you owned your own home wouldn't some of these problems happen anyway? Yes, but the problems of

renting can be avoided if you are the owner. If you own your own home you will be more responsive to the things that need attention because you will take pride in the ownership of your house. Let me take you back to the time where the lights in your rented apartment flickered for two hours and you were scared to death that the apartment might burn down. Heck, you didn't know anything about electricity. You only knew that your landlord was not answering the phone as you  were frantically calling to tell them that you were in the dark, wondering all the while how to finish preparing your half cooked meal that will not be ready for the gathering of friends now on their way. Your landlord seems to be "on vacation" with your rent money. I can go on and on about the experience of renting, in fact, I'll bet you could share with me some of your own renting nightmares. Let me ask you something... Are you still renting?

Why? Is it because you feel you must or do you think it's just the way things have to be?? Maybe your credit is not so great and that makes home ownership seem out of reach. Do you think owning your own place is just for the wealthy? What if the only thing holding you back is the fact that you don't know something that I do?

I know how to make this happen for you, even if you don't have good credit, even if you are filled with doubts about where and how to start the process of becoming a homeowner. It is time to get those limiting beliefs out of your head! Look, the world is changing and you can use that change to improve

your life for the better. You are reading this book to find answers to the limiting beliefs you always had about owning your own home. We all have had these thoughts of *"I can't,"* or *"I don't know,"* or *"Is my dream even possible?"* But you are reading this to learn how you can own your own home. I know what steps to take to start the process, and yes it is possible to own your own home. As a matter of fact, having your dream could be possible in 30 days or less. In fact, one phone call or email - yes one phone call or email right now could be your fast track to owning your very own American dream this month!

Imagine making this dream a reality. Admit it, you have always wanted to own your own home, but thought it was a goal just out of your reach. Listen, I know how it feels to be in a crowd of friends who are all talking about their new ownership stories, especially how much fun they have had with the latest DIY projects. Then, when the conversation  turns to you, all you can say is *"I'm a renter."* Your buddy just installed a beautiful new bathroom tile on his own and all you did was sign a check that helped send your landlord to the Bahamas! That feeling alone is enough to create the spark you need to make this happen for you.

What if you think you missed your opportunity, that this is just the wrong time for you to buy a house? That limiting belief is wrong! This is the magic time to take advantage of the housing market. We are at the bottom of the market and slowly climbing up. This is the opportune time to get yours.

Houses are selling for peanuts. If you have a line of credit, then go out and buy your home now. But if you are renting and the only thing standing between you and your own home is shaky credit, do not worry! You can still own your own home and I am going to show you how.

Listen, in my hometown right now in Franklin County, New York, there are not a lot of high paying jobs. Most of the manufacturing plants have shut down. General Motors (GM) has closed for good here. Just a few days ago it was announced that 1,000's more jobs in my area are in jeopardy because another manufacturer, an aluminum plant, could follow GM's suit. So I can relate to the income subject when people ask me, "Jay, how can I afford all the financing costs to even become a homeowner?" My clients ask me questions like, *"How do I come up with the 20% down the bank requires me to have?" "What if my mortgage payment is way more than my rental payment?" "What do I do about insurance, taxes, or paper work that comes with being a home owner?"* Again, don't worry, I will hold your hand and walk you through all of these scary questions and any more you may have.

Look, we are in a world of information. I am going to give you the key that unlocks the door to your own American Dream home. Now everyone's dream may be different, but doesn't everyone want a place of their own where they can raise a family, or be proud to gather with friends? Your dream may be a ranch style home, or it could be like that huge five bedroom farm house you grew up in. I don't know, but each of us can picture sitting next to grandma and grandpa in a nice warm cozy house, which we own, sharing stories and feeling the love

of family. It's hard to explain, but somehow, it's just not the same as gathering in a rented apartment.

This is what I know, as I said, the world is changing and getting back to our roots is something we need to do. Home ownership is at the top of everyone's dream list...

Are you sick and tired of renting and you don't know which way to turn? You have a good job, but don't know exactly how you are going to become a home owner. But you know it has to happen. Most people never figure it out. They never learned the path to take to become an owner.

Every renter's dream is owning a home, but not every renter has a system to make it happen. What if all that was holding that renter back is that he never found a mentor in someone that can lead him down the road to the American Dream. Most of you might be thinking those limiting thoughts, *"I can't."* or *"I don't know how."* What if you are just stuck and all you need is help with taking the right first step? Renters take life one day at a time, until they get fed up with renting, and all the hassles that go with it, like constantly calling their landlord to take care of problems. They finally get tired of people asking them where they live and having to answer "I live in a small 300 sq. ft. apartment."

Don't get me wrong, I had a lot of fun and memorable times in a small two bedroom mobile home, but I sure am grateful to have learned what it takes to be a homeowner.

It's tough when you don't know what to do.

Let me tell you, it's not easy these days to just know exactly what to do. So maybe you have made the decision, that now is

time to buy your own place, but you are plagued with questions. Where can I get the money to buy? Who do I ask for information? Why is it so tough to get answers? Those kinds of questions are what a lot of people are asking themselves.

I have talked with many renters and most of the time they say, "Jay, I don't know what rent-to-own is." "I have no clue about the first steps to take." Nearly all of my clients are just overwhelmed when they tell me "I don't have the money for a down payment."

ROADBLOCKS

What are the common obstacles or objections my clients are going to have?

1. I don't know the process.

2. How do I get the down payment?

3. Who can I trust to guide me?

4. What forms or contracts do I use?

5. I am afraid of what I don't know!

These are just a few of many roadblocks that we will address in a later chapter. Keep reading!

These People Didn't Let Any Of Those "Problems" Stop Them!!!

Let me introduce you to some amazing people who have overcome all those problems and obstacles that had previously kept them from homeownership.

These individuals used my expert advice to move beyond their fears, the "what ifs" that you probably also have, and now they are proud owners of their "own" home. Feel the excitement that they share.

I still remember the day we looked at "our" home. It was the middle of winter. We pulled up to the house with Jay. And I couldn't help but think "No way will this house ever be ours!!!

It was a big beautiful old farm house. Our dream home, big house, big garage, and a nice yard. We started looking around and we fell in love. We went home that night and talked about it.

We were in a beautiful 3 bedroom trailer but it was costing us $650 per month. We thought we could never do it. I called Jay to get the numbers from him. $5000 down and $477 a month. I thought "wow" we can do that. So I told him "Let's do it!". Three months later we were in our family's dream home. One we will never outgrow... Jay is a man of his words and he has been awesome to deal with. I now have my family's forever home.

Jason Noon

Or how about this lady, who writes:

My experience working with Jay St. Hilaire has been exceptional. Jay enabled my fiancé and I to purchase our dream home on a rent to own basis during a trying time for us. Jay is extremely knowledgeable, friendly, and professional. We would do it all over again. Thanks Jay.

Deb Williamson and Scott Shipman

I Was a Renter, Just Like You

I was no different from many of you. I had tried many times as a young adult to figure out how to own a home and it seemed liked it would never happen. I remember when it was a struggle to find the financing to buy something when I only had one income to use. To make things clear to you - I had more month at the end of my money. I remember thinking there has got to be a way to afford my own house! It can be upsetting sometimes to go through this and I remember those feelings.

It took me a long time to figure this stuff out. I applaud you for dedicating yourself, like I did, to learn how to make your dream of homeownership a reality.

Believe me, I have been exactly where you are right now. I went from renting one place to the next, while working, sometimes 70 hours per week, just to keep my eye on the goal of someday owning my own home. I could visualize myself sitting in my recliner with a hot cup of green tea in my hand, surrounded by my family, and just enjoying each other's company. I knew someday I would make it happen but more often than not, I would be snapped out of my "American Dream" by the coldness of my rented apartment.

Even now as I have owned many homes, I still remember the struggles and hardship of renting. Back then, I did not know anyone that had the answers to the questions I had. I only

knew that hard work would take care of everything. Each day I would tell myself that someday my hard work would pay off and I would be able to have a house to call my very own.

I did not know then what I know now, about a path and plan to get to home ownership, quickly and precisely. It is that path and my fail-proof plan that is going to help you achieve your dream of homeownership. Get ready for what you are about to learn!

I consider myself a life-long learner and I pride myself on listening to the best experts and mentors in any subject I want to learn more about.

It wasn't always like this though, I previously thought the only thing I need do, to experience the joys of life, was just work hard. After research, study and the benefit of my personal life experiences, I have come to know that hard work is not enough. It is important to work hard, learn and grow, but I found for me, the most important keys to living a fulfilled life are sharing, teaching, and inspiring others. This is why I am sharing this information with you. I want you to have something that you have always dreamed of- to achieve your goals. My dream of home ownership became a reality and I want this for you, too!

From Renter to Owner

Look, I have invested thousands of dollars in training and learned from the best real estate trainer in history.

Day in and day out, I studied properties and homes. I worked to translate that knowledge, into action, so I could learn what to do to own real estate. It has been my focused mission, over the last

Several years, to convert renters into home owners. I finally decided the reason I was put on this earth is to teach and inspire others, so I needed to keep learning about my passionate subject of real estate. I stopped worrying about having to know everything and started teaching what I have learned so far. I knew that others, like you, could benefit greatly from my experience, including how to avoid pitfalls that I now know are avoidable. I finally summoned the courage to write this book to outline for you, my proven blueprint to making you a property owner.

You see, I have acquired many homes throughout my learning career. Many I built with my dad and many others I acquired through the process I am about to show you. If you just stay with me for the rest of this journey, you can become a homeowner now, and who knows you, too, may own multiple homes - just like me. That is my dream for you. I finally cracked the code on this "rent to own" process and I am sharing it with you.

Myths Dispelled

So I finally succeeded in owning my own home, but you know what? You are probably thinking, "Yeah, sure Jay, you did it because you had help and the right people to learn from". You are thinking, and believing, in all these myths that others fill their minds with. Your mind is saying "it's easy for you or others to do this, but I can't." As a matter of fact these are the same things I said at one time. I thought heck, owning my own home will cost thousands of dollars, there is no way I will ever be able to afford this. Owning your own home is only for the rich. These are real thoughts that come into our minds when we "don't know, what we don't know." You know what? I learned that this not the case. At one time, I thought, wow, it will be hard to learn what to do in order to become a homeowner. I found out that this is not the case.

Believe me, not everyone is willing to share what they know. It's tough to find a mentor to take you by the hand and guide you through a process that improves your life. It takes patience and inspiration to learn anything new. But overcoming your fear of not knowing something and finding the right person to learn from can be intimidating. But I am here to show you something that can change your life. You can finally have ownership of your own home. I will show you exactly what to do, step by step.

Homeowner Blueprint

Finally, we are at the point you have been waiting for, so let's get right to it.

Let's overcome those roadblocks we discussed in Chapter 3.

Roadblock #1: I DON'T KNOW THE PROCESS.

Let's start with the very basics first, what is a "rent to own"? A "rent to own" is a process of selling or buying a property through certain terms and agreements that allow the parties to negotiate a purchase price, down payment and the monthly payment on a property. Both parties also agree to the length of time payments will be made. The agreement, or contract, is settled upon and written by an attorney. The buyers will bring the agreed upon down payment to closing. The first payment date will be mutually agreed upon and the buyers are expected to begin making payments from that date forward. An amortization (payment) schedule will be drawn up, which details the amount of money paid to principal and interest for all payments from the first to the last. This amortization is just like an amortized schedule you would get from the bank on any loan. The seller is responsible for providing this amortization document. Whether you are the buyer or the seller, you may be thinking this sounds too complicated. It's not; the attorney will take care of all of this- no worries!

For a detailed explanation of the "rent to own" concept, sometimes called "land contract," Google the term "land contract."

Roadblock #2: HOW DO I GET THE DOWN PAYMENT?

First- You may have access to funds you didn't know about. WHAT??? HOW???

1. Do you have an IRA, a 401k, or similar retirement fund?

2. Do you have a line of credit?

3. Do you have a savings account?

But, Jay, what if I do not have any of the above?

1. Do you have any liabilities? (What are liabilities? Liabilities are toys, or recreational vehicles; basically anything that you have that is valuable that you could "sell" to have your down payment for your "land contract" home.)

2. Do you have friends, or relatives that would let you borrow money?

3. Do you have items lying around that you could convert to cash by having yard sale?

Doing one or all of these things can help you accumulate the money you need for your down payment!

Contact a mortgage broker in your area. Google mortgage brokers near you. They can help you finance where banks will

not. Once you have your property, a broker might be a great asset. They may even help you build your credit to where you could "pay off" your rent to own "in full" with a mortgage.

Road Block #3: WHO CAN I TRUST TO GUIDE ME?

You will need to find a mentor or someone who has knowledge or experiences in rent to own. How, you ask? Search your area on the internet. A simple Google search with the terms "investor" or "rent to own" and the name of your area should help you find someone. You could also use your own social networking tools, like Facebook, or Craigslist for "rent to own." Send an email, or message to these new contacts. Ask them to meet you for coffee, or a drink of your choice, and discuss the rent to own process.

Another strategy for finding a mentor is to join forums, or internet sites that focus on the rent to own strategy. There are a lot of free sites that have potential mentors in their pages. Research them, read their posts, or blogs and pick the one who best fits your needs. I will be writing another book in the near future on how to find "your" mentor, so be on the lookout for that also! Sign up for my mailing list on www.jaysthilaire.com for tons of free information and training that is already available to you!

With the help of this book and your mentor's advice, you will be off and running!

Roadblock #4: WHAT FORMS OR CONTRACTS DO I USE?

Your attorney will handle all the necessary paperwork and contracts for you, whether you are buying or selling the

property. He or she will have all of the necessary forms and contracts for you. Do not worry!! Your attorney will have all the answers for you!

If you are savvy with the process, you can go to internet forums to research different contracts for rent to own. My mentor, Dean Graziosi, has a number of free contracts and documents on his free site at www.deangraziosi.com. You may sign up as a free member to access these items. Look on the left margin of the website for Forms and Documents. This site is also a place to network, learn and possibly find a mentor who will guide you through your learning process. This is precisely where I started learning about real estate, so I know you will be in good hands.

If you are not savvy about contracts, or the process, rely on your attorney. Do not "skimp" on this step. An experienced real estate attorney will save you both time and money. All real estate transactions must be recorded at your municipality's clerk's office- usually at the county level, and your attorney will file this for you. An Abstract, is a detailed history of each property. A search of this Abstract will look to see if any liens are held against the property. This is an example of why you want your attorney to assist you. Real estate deals have been stopped due to "hidden" issues like a lien that is held against the property. So, finding a good attorney can help you avoid pitfalls and save you in the long run.

Roadblock #5: I AM AFRAID OF WHAT I DON'T KNOW

This road block is also answered in Road Block #3, finding a mentor. This whole book should already be helping you

change your mind-set. If you are afraid of something, anything, I would suggest you "practice" facing the obstacle head on! Seek out and learn all you can about what you are afraid of. Believe me; I had many fears of not knowing what to do. Sometimes, you just don't know what you don't know. This book changes all of that and you are now in the "process" of changing your life and overcoming your fears!!!

Now that you have overcome these challenges, we are ready to take the first step in owning your own home:

1. Find an area, or neighborhood, you want to call home.

    a. This is no brainer. I am sure you already know this, but if you don't, one of the things you may want to consider, especially if you have children, is the school district. School district is key!

    b. Next, do you want to be in town or in the country? What amenities can you just not live without? Would you like to live close to stores, the post office, gas stations, library etc., or what about just close to nature?

    c. Then, you may want to think about driving distance to work or school.

2. Type of home

    a. Ranch

    b. 2 story

    c. manufactured (double wide or single wide)

3. Size

   a. 1 bedroom 1 bath?

   b. 2 bedroom 2 bath?

   c. 3 bedroom, with pool?

4. Lot or Landscape

   a. What size lot? Do you want wooded acres with a brook, no neighbors? Or do you want a safe neighborhood where the kids can ride their bikes with their friends?

   b. What would your landscape look like? Would you like a manicured lawn, with room for a garden, or would you prefer a small yard that would not take much time to mow?

5. Cost

   a. How much can I afford?

HERE IS WHERE YOU NEED TO CONCENTRATE!

Figure out your expenses.

Tally your current monthly bills. What do you pay each month on your car payment, insurance, loans, and credit cards? What is your current rental monthly payment? This step is a must. *Do Not Forget Anything!*

This process will show you what you have left at the end of the month. This is what I know: If you don't or haven't paid

attention to your finances, then now is the time. Don't leave out your rental payment, you are going to use this money to make your new home payment.

Car	$_____
Loan	$_____
Rental	$_____
Utilities	$_____

Or you can go to ask.com and you will find multiple worksheets for creating a monthly budget.

Here is something for you...

www.bettermoneyhabits.com

Another useful budget tool can be found at www.myfinances.com. There is www.monthlyexpensecalculator.com, as well. These are just a few websites that will help you establish a list of your expenses. If these don't suit you, you can Google *"monthly budget planner"* and find one that does. I am not endorsing any of these sites; I am just giving you examples to get you going in the right direction. Choose the one that best suits your needs and once that step is done, move to the next step!

NOTE: Property managers and landlords typically figure your income must be 3X your rent payment to allow you to qualify

to rent from them. (For example, if you currently pay $600 in rent each month, your income should be $1800 a month.) So, if your rent payment X 3 is more than what you currently have for a monthly income, then you need to increase your income. You may be able to find a seller willing to do a "no money down deal" and adjust the payments to fit your budget.

NOW you are ready to find a Seller. How??

Step 1

Search your area for RENT TO OWN HOMES. This will give you an idea of what is available.

a. Search Craigslist (www.craiglist.org,), then click on US (or whatever area you are in). Click your state (example: New York) or just click on your region (example: Syracuse). Then, under the heading "housing," click "real estate for sale". Scroll through and concentrate on "By Owner" ads. Look for other headings, like Rent to Own. If that is too many steps, you can just go back to the homepage of the region or area you are interested in and using the search feature, type "rent to own homes" under housing. This will list the available rent to own homes.

How else can you find rent to own homes?

- For sale by owner (FSBO) forsalebyowner.com

  - ☐ How else can you find FSBO's? Drive around the area you want to live and look for yard signs!

- Search for an investor that specializes in rent to owns.

- Pick up your local penny saver, free trader, or join your local online market

Zillow.com is another resource to find rent to own homes in your area. You can even Google the term "Rent to Own" to find available properties. Remember to include your area's name in your search!

IMPORTANT TIP: Opt into my rent to own page and get on my list for rent to own homes: www.jaysrenttoown.com.

- Be on the lookout for bandit signs- What are bandit signs? They are the 18" x 24" signs that are everywhere (in some towns) on telephone poles, in yards, or along the roads, mostly in high traffic areas like Walmart, McDonalds, and at intersections.

  Investors use these to market to buyers and sellers. They usually say: "I BUY HOUSES ANY CONDITION", or "FOR SALE 3 bedroom 2 bath Handyman Special". Call these numbers and begin to tell them you want a rent to own home.

- Post a "Rent to Own Wanted" ad on bulletin boards in local businesses. Gas stations, quick stops, banks, sandwich

shops, pharmacies, etc. are all places you might be able to attract a potential seller.

- Facebook – put your social network to good use. Tell your contacts you are looking for a rent to own property. Put it in your timeline. You can even start your own group and invite your investing mentors to join you.

Or find an "A" player Real estate agent...

TIP: www.jaysrenttoown.com

Once you find your home, you are going to have to negotiate the terms.

What does "terms" mean?? It means the

1. Down payment

2. Monthly payment

3. Total sale price

4. Interest rate

5. Length of contract

Example:

> *Total sale $45,000.00*
>
> *Down payment $5,000.00*
>
> *Monthly payment $382.26*
>
> *Interest 8%*
>
> *Length of contract 15 years*

These are all negotiated with the seller. When you call and ask questions of the seller, they may already have determined the "terms" they want, or they may have ballpark figures in mind. But remember everything is negotiable. People's needs, wants and minds change daily!! These are just some of the questions you may have, but these pages have answered the major ones you will need. Believe me when I was starting out just like you, I had hundreds of questions. Do not be afraid to ask. Remember your attorney will have answers. Your real estate agent is a good source of knowledge if they have used, studied or experienced rent to own situations.

Investors that specialize in rent to own properties would be great source of knowledge. Better yet, you can always access my website www.jaysthilaire.com for free training videos and tons of information available to you 24/7.

STEP 2

Find an Investor. This may be your single most important task to finding a rent to own home. I am an investor and pride myself on learning all I can about real estate and strive to teach and inspire anyone who is willing to learn. I believe

most investors yearn to get better and share all they know with buyers, sellers and team members. So, seek them out first! With this in mind, tap into their circle and absorb as much of their knowledge as you can to help you complete your newly signed deal.

If you have read this far, you are at the top 1% that will do what it takes to become a home owner. Let me give you a few ways to find investors that will help you all the way. That's right, all the way through this rent to own journey. Yes, you are finally going to be a homeowner. It's starting to feel real now isn't it?

How do you find your local investor?

a. Bandit signs. Bandit signs do not just advertise properties, they are also ways investors seek out new buyers.

b. Social networking- I cannot stress this enough, the old saying, "It's not what you know; it's who you know" is so true! Ask people in your circle of friends if they know of any investors in the area that specialize in rent to owns. Since becoming an investor, and using the very same strategies I am teaching you right now, I am certain there are people in your area that are willing to help you achieve your dream of homeownership- just like they helped me!

c. Log on to online search tools: Craigslist, Ask.com, Google, etc. Use the search term "investor" in the real estate sections. Call them and "interview" them about the properties they have listed, or about any properties they may know about. Ask your mentor!

I FOUND THE PROPERTY I WANT, NOW WHAT????

Do I draw up a contract on my own? Which one do I use?

a. Land Contract?

b. Contract for Deed?

c. Lease Option?

d. Option to Purchase?

These are all good choices. You might be asking, "But which one do I use?" Again, don't worry, your attorney will have the answers. If you still don't have an attorney, go to yp.com (yellow pages) and search for your town/city for an attorney who specializes in real estate. You may have to call a few, but be sure to tell them specifically you want to "rent to own a home" and you have a seller that you are now communicating with and you want to organize a contract and terms to complete the transaction.

Ask the attorney, "Can you do this?" Believe me; they will take you by the hand and do all the work it takes to handle the sale. Do not worry about it. You cannot know everything, you just to need to know who to ask and your real estate attorney will take care of the rest.

TIP* Not all attorneys specialize in rent to owns. You may have to call a few, maybe three, or even six to find the one that specializes in real estate transactions. Remember you are looking for someone to help you finally achieve your

homeownership dreams, so searching for a knowledgeable attorney that knows his or her "stuff" is worth the effort!

But, Jay, this sounds like a really good plan, but why am I doing this? Why should you become a homeowner?

Here are 10 reasons:

1. Pride

2. Equity

3. Own the American Dream

4. Appreciation

5. Security

6. No Private Mortgage Insurance (PMI) payments

7. Gain self-worth

8. Lower Down Payment

9. Work with an expert

10. Fixed rates (monthly payments)

There are even more very important added bonuses of rent to own homeownership: You don't have to have perfect credit!

No hassle from landlords!

You get to live and do as you please!!!

After reading this book and taking action on each of these steps, if you still can't find an investor to help you in your area, opt into my website at jaysrenttoown.com or www.jaysthilaire.com.

Are you ready? Do you think you can do this? I know you can because I have done this. I have helped my friends and family members do this and YOU CAN, TOO!!! Get out there! Get a mentor! Find the home of your dreams! You have earned it!

Tips for Success

If you are going to realize the American Dream of homeownership then you have to focus on answering the questions I have outlined prior.

The main ones being:

1. Where do I want to own? What area?

2. How much do I have or can I get for a down payment?

3. What can I afford for a monthly payment?

After you have answered these top 3 questions then you must start the process by finding an investor in your area that specializes in rent to owns.

You must become serious about taking these steps to become a homeowner and stop procrastinating. The knowledge you have acquired in these pages will eliminate your fear and finally end your renting days. Make sure you look carefully for an expert in "Rent to Owns" in your area.

If you need an expert to guide you or find a rent to own home in your area then go to www.jaysrenttoown.com and contact me.

If you know someone who must sell or is losing their home, go to: www.jayhousebuyers.com

Do This Today

Your first action step today is to act.

Take all the information I gave you and decide you are going to become a homeowner. If you don't decide, then all of what you have just read will be of little value to you.

My #1 goal of writing this Book is to give you the best information to make you a homeowner, now!! I want to serve you and I care about giving you the tools and knowledge to make it happen.

NOW DO THIS TODAY

#1 - Find an investor in your wanted area and contact them.

EXAMPLE: yp.com *"rent to own"* or go to my site www.jaysrenttoown.com to be on my list.

#2 - Give them all your criteria of where you want to live, what size house, bed, bath, lot size, and what you need included.

#3 - Let them know what you have for a down payment, what you can afford for a monthly payment and negotiate the purchase price.

#4 - The investor will take it from there!!!

THAT'S IT!!!

www.ingramcontent.com/pod-product-compliance
Lightning Source LLC
Chambersburg PA
CBHW070925180526
45168CB00005B/2162